Pie Iron Cookbook: 60 #Delish Pie Iron Recipes for Cooking in the Great Outdoors

RHONDA BELLE

DEDICATION

To Foodies Everywhere...Enjoy & Be Well!

Table of Contents

ACKNOWLEDGEMENTS

To the love of my life, Johnny.
You are Mommy's greatest inspiration.

To my Mom & Dad (Sunset February 2016).
Love you always...

Easy As Pie!

Make your next outdoor experience even better with a tasty dish cooked over an open flame! Pie irons are convenient, fun and easy to use.

Cast iron pie makers need to be seasoned just like cast iron skillets. To do this, coat the skillet with cooking oil and bake it in a 350° F oven for an hour. Wipe well with paper towels when done. Aluminum pie makers do not need this type of seasoning, but most people prefer cast iron pie irons for their durability and heat conductivity. They can be heavier than aluminum however, so if hiking, plan accordingly.

The basic method for making pie iron sandwich dishes is to preheat the iron over hot coals. Butter the outsides of two bread slices or a pie pastry and lightly spray pie iron with nonstick cooking spray. Place the buttered sides against the pie iron. Add desired fillings (pre-cooked meats unless the recipe states otherwise) and close and latch the pie iron. Place the pie iron over glowing coals, flipping occasionally. In 2-10 minutes enjoy a delicious treat. *Be careful! Fillings will be extremely hot so cut up pies for the little ones and allow them to cool before serving.*

There are many items that can be prepared in a pie iron, including savory sandwiches, pizza pies, omelets, French toast, s'mores, grilled cheese, waffles, burgers and more. Options are endless, so try these 60 super recipes on your next camping or outdoor adventure!

Bacon, Egg & Cheese Pudgy

1 fresh egg
2 slices of bread
Nonstick cooking spray
Strips of uncooked bacon (desired amount)
Spray pie iron with nonstick cooking spray. Next, cut bacon strips in half and lay them in the pie iron. Set 1 slice of bread on top of the bacon. Gently pat down the bread. Crack egg onto the bread. Lay cheese over top and cover with the other slice of bread. Close and cook slowly. When the bacon is cooked, the egg inside will be cooked as well. #Delish!

Beef Stew Brew

Pie pastry
Canned beef stew
Nonstick cooking spray
Spray iron to prevent food from sticking. Place pie pastry on ½ of iron and spoon stew in center. Top with additional pastry. Close cooker, latch, trim excess pastry and cook until golden brown. #Delish!

Berry Blue French Toast

¼ cup fresh blueberries
½ teaspoon vanilla
1 large egg
1 tablespoon milk
2 tablespoons cream cheese, softened
4 slices of bread
Nonstick cooking spray
Coat pie iron with nonstick cooking spray. In a bowl, smash blueberries into the softened cream cheese. Spread two slices of bread with the cream cheese mixture. Top each slice with another bread slice. In another bowl, beat the egg with the milk and vanilla. Dip each side of the sandwiches into the egg mixture. Place the French toast sandwiches inside pie ion. Close and cook each side for a few minutes until bread is golden brown. #Delish!

Berry Blue Turnover

2 slices whole wheat bread
3 tablespoons canned blueberry pie filling
Margarine or butter
Sugar

Spread margarine on bread. Put one slice, buttered side down, on one side of the pie iron. Put pie filling in the middle of the slice of bread. Place the other side of bread, buttered side up, on top of the filling. Close iron and latch shut. Remove any excess bread hanging over the side. Place pie iron over coals or open flames, checking every couple minutes. Remove from heat when bread is the desired color of toasted brown. Plate and sprinkle with sugar to serve. Enjoy!

Best of Brie

Prepared pie pastry
Nonstick cooking spray
Small brie cheese wheel (or cut up a larger wheel to fit pie iron)
Sun-dried tomatoes

Generously spray both halves of the pie iron. Place piece of pie pastry in ½ of iron. Place brie in center and top with sun-dried tomatoes. Top with piece of pie pastry. Close iron, latch and trim excess pastry. Grill until golden brown. Serve with fresh apple slices and white wine. #Delish!

Bleu Club

2 slices of bread
Deli sliced ham
Deli sliced turkey breast
Precooked bacon strips, cut in half
Margarine or butter
Swiss cheese

Butter bread slices and place one on each side of pie iron. Place slices of turkey breast, ham, bacon, and Swiss cheese on one side. Close iron and latch; place in red coals, cooking until the filling starts to bubble, and the cheese has melted. Enjoy!

BLT Deluxe

2 slices of bread
Butter or margarine
Cheddar cheese slices
Mayo
Precooked bacon strips
Shredded lettuce
Tomato slices

Butter the outsides of the bread. Spread the mayo on the un-buttered side of one slice of bread. Place bacon, tomato and cheese slices on bread. Top with remaining piece of bread. Close iron (buttered sides against pie iron), latch and trim any excess bread. Grill until golden brown. #Delish!

Bodacious Burrito Pudgy Pie

Burrito size tortillas
Grilled onions and bell peppers, chopped
Nonstick cooking spray
Prepared taco meat
Salsa
Shredded cheddar cheese

Pre-prepare taco meat at home; place in zip-lock bags and store in a cooler. At the camp, place a large tortilla into a lightly sprayed pie iron. *The tortilla will cover both sides of the open pie iron. Place ingredients on one side only.* Filling will be 2 tablespoons of taco meat, a spoon of salsa, cheddar cheese and a few onions and peppers. Fold the burrito in half and fold in the edges to make a square packet. Close the pie iron and cook for about 3 minutes on each side until tortilla turns golden. Add salsa and enjoy!

Bountiful Bacon Burger

¼ cup of precooked hamburger, crumbled
2 slices of bread
Butter or margarine
Favorite cheese slices
Pre-cooked, bacon strips

Butter the outsides of the bread. Place meat and cheese in the center of a slice of bread and top with remaining slice. Close pie iron, latch, trim any excess bread, and cook until golden brown. Enjoy!

Campsite Chicken Pot Pie

1 can cream of chicken soup
1 can mixed vegetables, drained
1 teaspoon chicken bouillon granules
2 tubes of Pillsbury big crescent rolls
6 ounces grilled chicken breast strips
Butter-flavored cooking spray
Salt and pepper to taste

In a sealable container, mix the grilled chicken breast strips, soup, vegetables and chicken bouillon. Add salt and pepper to taste. Keep refrigerated or in a cooler until needed. Spray the pie iron well cooking spray. On a plate, roll out the crescent roll package into flat triangles. Place 1/3 cup of the chicken mixture on top of the laid out crescent roll in the pie iron. Cover the mixture with another crescent roll. Seal the edges by pressing down on the dough. Close iron and place near campfire coals. Cook each side about 2 minutes or until nicely toasted. Slide onto a plate. Let cool. #Delish!

Cherry Cheesecake Pastry

1 can cherry pie filling
2 slices of bread (or pie pastry)
Cream cheese
Margarine or butter
Mini marshmallows

Butter outsides of bread. Spread softened cream cheese onto both pieces of bread. Spoon pie filling onto center of bread and top with marshmallows. Add other bread slice to make a sandwich. Close iron, latch, trim any excess bread and grill until golden brown. #Delish!

Chicken BBQ Pudgy Pie

2 slices Italian bread
Bulls Eye BBQ sauce
Precooked chicken breast, thinly sliced
Margarine or butter
Shredded Monterrey Jack
Sliced Canadian bacon

Butter outsides of bread. Place the chicken, BBQ sauce, Canadian bacon, and shredded cheese between bread slices. Close iron (buttered sides against pie iron), latch and trim any excess bread. Grill until golden brown. #Delish!

Cinnamon-Apple Adventure

1 can apple pie filling
Cinnamon & sugar to taste
Golden raisins
Tube of crescent rolls (or pie pastry)
Powdered sugar
Nonstick cooking spray

Mix pie filling, cinnamon, sugar and raisins. Spray both halves of iron with nonstick cooking spray. Place crescent roll in one side of iron and spoon apple mixture in center. Top with second crescent roll square. Close iron, latch, trim any excess dough and cook until golden brown. Dust with powdered sugar when done. Enjoy!

Classic PB&J

Butter or margarine
2 slices of bread
Peanut butter
Your favorite jam or jelly

Butter outsides of bread. Spread peanut butter and jam on unbuttered side of bread slices and place in cooker. Close and latch iron, trimming any excess. Grill until golden brown. Enjoy!

Cream Cheese Delights

2 slices honey wheat bread
Precooked bacon, crumbled
Slices of fresh tomato
Softened vegetable flavored cream cheese spread
Spread margarine or nonstick butter spray

Butter or spray outside of bread. Spread thin layer of cream cheese on each inside piece of bread. Sprinkle crumbled bacon on top of the cream cheese on one bread slice and top with one slice of tomato. *The tomato slice should have some of the moisture taken out with a paper towel.* Place other slice of bread on top. Close pie iron and cook in campfire until golden brown. #Delish!

Creative Chicken Cordon Bleu

1 can of mushroom soup, undiluted
2 slices of bread
Deli-sliced chicken breast
Deli-sliced ham
Margarine or butter
Nonstick cooking spray
Sour cream
Swiss cheese slices
White wine

Spray pie iron. Combine one tablespoon of sour cream with one tablespoon mushroom soup. Add 1 teaspoon of white wine (pour yourself a drink with the rest). Prepare bread as usual. Place chicken and ham slices on bread and top with Swiss cheese and sour cream/mushroom soup mixture. Top with remaining piece of bread. Close iron (buttered sides against iron), latch and trim any excess bread. Grill until golden brown. #Delish!

Easy Egg Delight

1 fresh egg, beaten
Cooked ham, chopped
Cooked or canned white potato, sliced
Grated cheddar cheese
Nonstick cooking spray
Onion and green pepper, chopped
Salt and Pepper

Spray both sides of iron with cooking spray. Layer 4 slices of cooked or can potato. Place egg mixture over sliced potatoes. Cook over campfire for 8 minutes potato side down. Turn over for 5 minutes more to cook egg. Enjoy!

Egg & Salmon Sammie

1 can salmon
1 fresh egg
2 slices of bread
2 slices wheat bread
2 tablespoons milk
Mayo
Nonstick cooking spray
Onion, finely chopped

Mix salmon, mayo and onion to make salmon salad. Mix egg and milk. Spray both side of iron with vegetable oil spray. Dip bread slices into egg mixture and place one slice in ½ of iron. Place salmon salad in center and top with remaining slice bread. Close iron, latch & trim any excess bread. Grill until golden on both sides. #Delish!

Forest Fried Potatoes

1 teaspoon butter or margarine
Green onions, chopped
Nonstick cooking spray
Parmesan cheese
Salt and pepper to taste
White potatoes, sliced or chopped

Prepare iron with cooking spray. Place potatoes and onions in iron, add butter, salt and pepper (to taste) and close. Grill on both sides over low heat. Remove from coals, plate and sprinkle liberally with Parmesan cheese. #Delish!

Fruity French Toast

2 fresh eggs, beaten
2 slices of wheat bread
Nonstick cooking spray
Strawberry jam or jelly

Dip 2 bread slices into egg batter, place both slices into a pie iron that has been sprayed with cooking spray. Place a spoonful of strawberry jam between the bread slices. Toast until browned. #Delish!

Great Garlic Biscuits

¼ teaspoon salt
1 can buttermilk biscuits
1 teaspoon garlic
Melted butter
Nonstick cooking spray

Spray iron with vegetable oil spray. Open biscuits and separate. Cut biscuits in half and shape into balls. Put a biscuit ball in melted butter blended with the garlic and cook in a pie iron until golden brown. Enjoy!

Greek Pudgy

2 slices of fresh bread
Butter or margarine
Feta cheese, crumbled
Mozzarella
Pitted black and/or green olives
Precooked chicken breast, chopped
Small jar of marinated artichokes, drained

Butter outsides of bread. Place chicken, cheeses, olives and artichokes in center of bread. Top with remaining bread slice. Close iron (buttered sides against pie iron), latch and trim any excess bread. Grill until golden brown. #Delish!

Grilled Gobblers

2 slices of bread
Butter or margarine
Deli-sliced turkey breast
Swiss cheese slices
Thousand Island dressing

Butter outsides of bread. Spread the salad dressing on the un-buttered side of one slice of bread. Place turkey slices and one slice of cheese on bread. Top with remaining piece of bread. Close iron (buttered sides against pie iron), latch and trim any excess bread. Grill until golden brown. #Delish!

Grilled Onion Overture

Celery salt to taste
Nonstick cooking spray
Parsley to taste
Sweet Vidalia onions
Wine or Beer

Place thinly sliced onions into pie iron. Add celery salt, parsley and a splash of white wine or beer. Close iron and grill until onions are soft and fragrant. Enjoy as is or use atop other grilled meats.

Grilled Roast Beef for Couples

½ tablespoon Dijon mustard
1 tablespoon mayo
2 slices Swiss cheese
4 slices bread
4 thin slices of roast beef (or left over steak)
Nonstick cooking spray
Salsa or picante sauce

Combine mayonnaise and mustard. Spray nonstick cooking spray in pie iron. Place bread in iron. Spread the mayo/mustard mixture on top and place two beef slices and one slice of cheese on bread. Top with a bit of salsa and the second slice of bread. Close iron, latch and trim any excess bread. Grill until golden brown. #Delish!

Grilled Roast Beef Sandwiches

1 can (4 ounces) green chilies, chopped
1 tablespoon Dijon mustard
10 cooked roast beef, thin or deli sliced
10 slices rye bread
2 tablespoon butter, softened
2 tablespoons mayonnaise (not Miracle Whip®)
5 slices Swiss cheese
Butter or margarine
Salsa or Picante Sauce

Combine chilies, mayonnaise and mustard. Butter one side of each slice of bread; place bread, buttered side down in pie iron. Spread about 1 tablespoon of chili mixture on non-buttered side of bread. Top half of the chili mixture with one slice of cheese and two slices of beef. Close pie iron and cook over fire until golden brown. #Delish!

Grilled Salmon Sandwich

1 can of salmon (or tuna), prepared as preferred
2 slices of bread
4 or 5 eggs, beaten
Favorite mayonnaise
Nonstick cooking spray
Onion powder
Salt and pepper

Make salmon/tuna salad, spread on one slice of bread and create a sandwich using the other piece of bread. Spray the inside of the pie iron; dip sandwich in eggs and place in pie iron. Cook and latch; place in fire. Flip occasionally until well toasted. Enjoy!

Hearty Havana Sandwiches

2 slices rye bread
Deli-sliced, ham
Flat sandwich-style pickles
Precooked pork meat, thinly sliced or chopped
Prepared mustard
Swiss cheese slices

Butter outsides of bread. Spread the mustard on the un-buttered side of one slice of bread. Place meat, pickle and cheese slices on bread, topping off with the remaining piece of bread. Close iron (buttered sides against the pie iron), latch and trim any excess bread. Grill until golden brown. Enjoy!

Hot Hobo Pot Pie

1 can brown gravy
1 can mixed vegetables, drained
1 package deli style chicken or turkey
2 slices of fresh bread
Butter or margarine

Butter one side of 1 slice of bread butter and place buttered side down in pie iron. Place 1 teaspoon of mixed vegetables onto bread. Put the desired amount of meat on bread; spoon gravy on top. Butter one side of another slice of bread and place it butter side up on top of meat/veggie/gravy mix. Seal up pie iron and place on hot coals. Cook for about 3 minutes per side depending on how hot the coals are. Remove and cool. #Delish!

Incredible Crab Sammie

Canned crab or crab flavored Pollock flakes
Cream cheese, brie or camembert cheese
Diced onions
2 slices of bread
Nonstick cooking spray

Spray pie iron to prevent sticking. Place crab, cheese and onion between bread slices. Close iron, latch and trim any excess bread. Grill until golden brown. #Delish!

Lemon Meringue Pie

1 can lemon pie filling
2 large marshmallows
2 slices of bread
Nonstick cooking spray

Spray iron. Spread lemon pie filling onto bread and top with marshmallows. Make sandwich using the other piece of bread. Place in pie iron, close, latch, trim any excess bread and grill until golden brown. #Delish!

Mighty Mushroom Melt

Butter or olive oil spray
Large portabella mushroom cap
Salt and pepper to taste
Slab of mozzarella cheese

Generously butter each half of the pie iron. Place the mushroom cap between the irons and sear over the fire for 2-3 minutes on each side. Open the irons and place a slab of mozzarella cheese on the underside of the mushroom cap. Close the irons and cook over glowing coals for a couple of minutes until the cheese is melted. Enjoy!

Monkey Butter Pudgy

Chocolate chips or Hershey's chocolate bar
Large banana, sliced
Mini marshmallows
Nonstick cooking spray or butter
Nonstick cooking spray or squeezable butter
Peanut butter
White bread

Butter or spray on one side of the pie iron or butter bread. Place one slice of bread on pie iron. Spread peanut butter on bread. Add banana, chocolate and marshmallows. Close iron and latch shut. Place in coals for about 4 minutes, flipping half-way through. Remove and serve hot. #Delish!

Outrageous Oatmeal Cakes

¼ teaspoon cinnamon
¼ teaspoon nutmeg
½ cup dry milk
1 egg (optional)
1 teaspoon baking powder
1¼ cup water
2 cups oatmeal (not instant)
2 tablespoon brown sugar
2 tablespoon oil
Nonstick cooking spray

Combine all the dry ingredients in a plastic baggie at home; include oil in a small plastic bottle. At the camp, spray both halves of iron with vegetable oil spray. Beat egg, oil, water and dry ingredients together. Let stand for 10 minutes – *very important.* Cook in a lightly sprayed iron until lightly browned. Serve with honey, butter, jam or syrup. #Delish!

PB & Banana Pudgy Pie

½ medium banana, sliced
1 sheet pre-made bread dough
2 tablespoons crunchy peanut butter
Nonstick cooking spray

Lightly spray both sides of the pie iron with the cooking spray. Lay the dough horizontally and cut in half. Take one half, fold in half lengthwise and spread on peanut butter. Place on one side of the pie iron. Layer on sliced banana. Fold other half of the dough lengthwise and lay on top of bananas. Close pie iron. Cook on campfire a couple minutes on each side being careful not to burn the dough. Remove and allow to cool. #Delish!

Peach Turnovers

¼ teaspoon nutmeg
¼ teaspoon sugar
2 slices of bread (or use crescent rolls or pie pastry)
Butter or margarine
Fresh and ripe peach slices
Powdered sugar
Pumpkin pie mix
Butter outsides of bread. Spoon pie mix, nutmeg, sugar, and peaches onto center of bread. Close cooker and latch. Trim excess dough and cook until golden brown. Dust with the powdered sugar. #Delish!

Perfect Peanut Butter Cup

2 slices of white bread
Peanut butter
Chocolate chips
Large marshmallow
Butter or margarine
Butter outsides of bread. Spread peanut butter and large marshmallow onto bread and top with chocolate chips. Close iron (buttered sides against iron), latch, trim any excess bread and grill until golden brown. #Delish!

Philly Cheesesteak

2 slices of Italian bread
Leftover steak from dinner, thinly sliced
Finely chopped onions, pepper and mushrooms
Slice of cheese (your choice…mozzarella, provolone, cheddar, Swiss, etc.)
BBQ sauce
Nonstick cooking spray
Spray iron and place bread inside. Add meat, onion, pepper & mushroom mixture, cheese and sauce in center of one slice of bread and top with remaining slice of bread. Close cooker, latch, trim excess bread and cook until golden brown. #Delish!

Pie Iron Cheesy Tots

1/3 teaspoon garlic salt
Cheddar cheese, shredded
Nonstick cooking spray
Salt and pepper, to taste
Tater tots
White onion and green peppers, chopped

Spray pie iron. Season tater tots and add veggies. Place in pie iron, latch closed and cook over glowing coals for 4-5 minutes. Remove, plate and add cheese, allowing it to melt. Enjoy!

Pie Iron Pizza

2 slices of bread
2 tablespoons pizza sauce
Margarine or butter
Precooked meat, such as lean hamburger or ham
Shredded mozzarella cheese
Sliced veggies of choice (i.e., mushrooms, green pepper, etc.)
Spread margarine on bread. Put one slice, buttered side down, on one side of the pie iron. Put pizza sauce, meat, veggies, and cheese in the middle of the slice of bread. Place the other side of bread, buttered side up, on top of the filling. Close pie iron and latch shut. Trim any excess bread outside of the pie iron. Place pie iron over coals or flames, checking every couple minutes. Remove from heat when bread is the desired color of toasted brown. #Delish

Pie Iron Reuben

1 slice Swiss cheese
1-2 spoonfuls of Thousand Island dressing
2 slices rye bread, outsides buttered
2-3 slices corned beef
2-3 spoonfuls of canned sauerkraut (*remember the can opener!*)
Butter or margarine
Place bread buttered side down on one side of the pie iron. Layer ingredients. Top with second slice of bread. Close iron and cook slowly over glowing coals for about five minutes. Enjoy!

Pie Iron Sloppy Joes

1 can sloppy joe mix
1 lb. cooked ground beef
2 slices of bread
Butter or margarine
Cheese slices
Prepare Sloppy Joe mix and ground beef at home and store in plastic container or zip-lock bags: place in cooler. When ready to cook, butter both slices of bread, add cheese of your choice and sloppy joe mixture. Cook over campfire until toasty and warm. #Delish!

Pie Iron Taco Party

½ cup chopped onion
1 (1 ounces) package taco seasoning mix
1 (8 ounces) container sour cream
1 (8 ounces) jar salsa
1 cup shredded Monterey Jack cheese
1 large tomato, diced
1 lb. precooked and taco-seasoned ground beef
12 (5-inch) corn tortillas
2 cups iceberg lettuce, shredded
Nonstick cooking spray

Spray the inside of a pie iron with cooking spray, and place a corn tortilla on one side. Place a scoop of ground beef on top of the tortilla, sprinkle with Monterey Jack cheese, and chopped onion. Finally, place another tortilla on top, and close the pie iron. Cook the taco over campfire until the tortillas have crisped and browned, and the taco is hot in the center. Serve with lettuce, tomato, salsa, and sour cream. #Delish!

Pizzeria Calzone

Butter or margarine
Cooked spinach
Jar white pasta sauce
Minced garlic
Nonstick cooking spray
Onion, chopped
Pillsbury pizza crust dough
Shredded mozzarella cheese
Sliced mushrooms

Prep pie iron with cooking spray. In ½ of pie iron, sauté onion, mushrooms and garlic in butter until tender. Top sautéed veggies with piece of pizza dough. Close cooker, turn pie over and open (you should see sautéed veggies on top). Place spinach and cheese in center of dough. Spoon pasta sauce over and top with another piece of pizza dough. Close and latch cooker. Trim excess dough. Grill until golden brown. Enjoy!

Quesadilla Pudgy Pie

¼ cup refried beans
¼ cup salsa
¼ cup shredded Monterrey Jack cheese
2 (5-inch) corn tortillas
Nonstick cooking spray

Lightly spray both sides of the pie iron with cooking spray. Place a corn tortilla on one side of the pie iron. Place refried beans inside of the tortilla and sprinkle with shredded cheese. Layer on the other tortilla and close pie iron. Cook the quesadilla in the campfire until the tortillas are slightly toasted. Serve with salsa. #Delish!

S'mores Sammies

¼ cup miniature marshmallows
2 slices of bread
2 tablespoons milk chocolate chips
2 tablespoons peanut butter
2 teaspoons butter or margarine

Spread butter onto one side of each slice of bread. Place bread butter sides down in the pie iron. Spread half of the peanut butter onto the exposed side of each piece of bread. Stick the marshmallows to one side and the chocolate chips to the other. Close the pie maker. Roast over a campfire for about 3 minutes on each side, until the bread is toasted with chips melted and marshmallows gooey. #Delish!

Samosa Pie

2 slices of bread
Butter or margarine
Canned peas and carrots
Curry powder
Leftover baked potato, diced
Precooked chicken, diced

Butter outsides of bread. Mix chicken, curry powder (to taste) and vegetables and place in center of bread. Top with remaining piece of bread. Close iron (buttered sides against pie iron), latch and trim any excess bread. Grill until golden brown. #Delish!

Seasoned Hash Browns

¼ cup shredded cheddar
½ avocado, roughly chopped
1 tomato, thinly sliced
2 cups hash brown potatoes
Nonstick cooking spray
Pinch of cayenne pepper
Salt and pepper, to taste
Coat pie iron with cooking spray and fill each half with about ¼ cup hash browns, packing them in. Top each side with cheese. Arrange tomato and avocado on one side and sprinkle with seasonings. Close the iron and cook on each side for a few minutes until hash browns are golden brown. #Delish!

Sumptuous Smoky Salmon

Brie or camembert cheese
Butter or margarine
Fresh or smoked salmon, thinly sliced
Sweet onion, thinly sliced
2 slices of bread
Butter outsides of bread. Place salmon, onion and cheese between bread slices. Close pie iron (buttered sides against iron), latch & trim any excess bread. Grill until golden on both sides. #Delish!

Sunrise McMuffins

½ cup cheese
1 lb. precooked sausage patties
1 package English muffins, split in half
2 tablespoons milk
8-10 fresh eggs, scrambled
Butter or nonstick cooking spray
Salt & pepper to taste
Butter or spray side of muffin, put butter side toward iron, then start to layer ingredients: sausage patty, a little egg (it will run but set when cooked), cheese sprinkles and topped with other muffin that has been buttered as well. Cook over campfire until sausage and egg are set. #Enjoy!

Super Steak Pasties

Butter
Cooked potato, cooked or sliced
Cooked steak, cooked
McCormick's Italian seasoning
Nonstick cooking spray
Onions, sliced
Pie pastry

Spray both iron halves with vegetable oil spray. Place pie pastry in ½ of iron. Place steak, potatoes and onions in center. Add a pat of butter and sprinkle with Italian seasoning. Place second piece of pastry over fillings. Close and latch cooker. Trim excess pastry. Grill until golden brown. #Delish!

Sweet Camping Dessert

2 slices of bread
Butter or margarine
Canned apples, blueberries, or cherries
Canned cake icing of choice (vanilla always works well)

Butter both sides of bread (these will touch the pie iron). Add fruit and close pie iron. Cook over fire with bright coals for no more than five minutes, flipping once. When done, remove from fire and carefully top with the canned icing. Enjoy!

Sweet Cinnamon Pie

Butter or margarine
Chocolate chips
Chopped walnuts
Cinnamon & sugar mixture to taste
Mini marshmallows
Nonstick cooking spray
Raisins
Tube of crescent rolls

Spray iron. Place one crescent roll square on iron. Place a pat of butter in center & pour a generous amount of cinnamon/sugar mixture, nuts, marshmallows and raisins onto 1 half and cover with another crescent roll square. Close & latch pie iron, trimming excess dough. Grill until crescent roll dough is done. #Delish!

Terrific Tuna Melt

1 small can tuna (*remember can opener*)
2 slices of bread
Butter
Cheese slices of choice
Chopped pickle
Dash Dijon mustard
Mayonnaise
Tomato slices
Mix tuna, pickle, mayo, and mustard (or use your own tuna salad recipe). Butter bread. Place tuna salad, a slice of cheese and a slice of tomato between bread. Close iron (buttered sides against iron), latch & trim any excess bread. Grill until golden on both sides. #Delish!

Tomato-Basil Panini

2 slices of white or Italian bread
Basil, chopped or freeze dried
Nonstick cooking spray
Salt to taste
Several mozzarella cheese slices
Tomato, sliced
Spray pie iron. Place a slice of bread topped with a slice of mozzarella, tomato, and basil in one side; add another slice of mozzarella on top. Sprinkle lightly with salt, place in pie iron and cook until grilled. Enjoy!

Turtle Pie

3 caramels per pie
Chocolate chips
Nonstick cooking spray
Tube of crescent rolls
Spray iron. Place one crescent roll square on iron. Place caramels, chocolate chips and marshmallows in center and cover with another crescent roll square. Close & latch cooker. Trim excess dough and grill until crescent roll dough is done. #Delish!

Veal Parmesan Sandwich

2 slices of bread
Mozzarella cheese
Nonstick cooking spray
Parmesan cheese
Pizza sauce
Precooked veal cutlet, sliced

Spray pie iron. Spread the pizza sauce on one slice of bread. Place meat slices on bread and sprinkle with parmesan and mozzarella cheeses. Top with remaining piece of bread. Close iron, latch and trim any excess bread. Grill until golden brown. #Delish!

World's Greatest Ham & Cheese

2 slices of bread
2-3 slices of deli ham
Butter or margarine
Favorite cheese slices
Spicy brown mustard

Butter outsides of bread. Spread the mustard on the un-buttered side of one slice of bread. Place ham slices and slice of cheese on bread. Top with remaining piece of bread. Close iron (buttered sides against pie iron), latch and trim any excess bread. Grill until golden brown. Enjoy!

Yesterday's Meatloaf Sandwich

1 slice of meatloaf
1 slice of onion
1 slice tomato
1 slice your favorite cheese
2 slices of whole grain bread
Butter or nonstick cooking spray

Prepare bread as usual. Layer meat, cheese, tomato and onion between slices of bread. Close and latch cooker. Trim excess bread. Grill until golden brown. #Delish!

Thank you for your purchase!
May you enjoy and be well!

ABOUT THE AUTHOR

I am a Tennessee native and a connoisseur of good eats. My culinary delights are inspired by my Southern roots.

I am from cornbread and cabbage, fried chicken and Kool-Aid soaked lemon slices.

I am from hen houses, persimmon trees and juicy, red tomatoes on the vine.

I am from sunflowers growing wild in summer and homemade ice cream in the winter.

I am from family reunions, blue collar men, happy housewives, and Sunday dinners.

I am from spiritual folks who didn't always get it right, but believed in the power of prayer – and taught it to their kids.

I am from the hottest of hot summers and kids running barefoot and free through thirsty Tennessee grass.

I am from a grandmother who sang gospel that was magic...song drenched air would tumble from her lungs, leap into your spirit and make you feel fantastic things.

I am from hard, heartfelt lessons about living and kitchens full of the perfume of love.

♥♥♥ *This book is from my heart to yours.* ♥♥♥

For info, freebies & new book notices, follow @SoDelishDish on social media!
Scan with your smartphone!

FIND MORE BOOKS ONLINE

19650131R00017